# INGRID MICHAELSON
## Everybody

This book was approved by Ingrid Michaelson

CD art design by Mikey Please, www.mikeyplease.co.uk

Piano/vocal arrangements by John Nicholas and Steven Burks

Cherry Lane Music Company
Director of Publications/Project Editor: Mark Phillips

ISBN 978-1-60378-226-5

*Visit our website at www.cherrylaneprint.com*

# INGRID MICHAELSON

## Everybody

"This was my big girl record," declares Ingrid Michaelson of 2009's *Everybody*, her second full-length CD. "It was almost a loss of innocence. I was 29 years old and I shouldn't have worried if my mom and dad knew that I kissed a boy from listening to one of my songs; but I remember on my first album I was like, 'Can I say that?' "

On that first album, 2007's critically lauded *Girls and Boys*, the singer/songwriter infiltrated the mainstream airways with smart love songs like "The Way I Am," a single that has gone on to sell over one million copies worldwide. With *Everybody*, she brings a newfound wisdom and maturity to her music, gleaned from touring the world. "This album is very autobiographical; it's about the past year and a half of my life and choices that I've made," Michaelson says. "I had other songs that weren't about that and I purposely didn't put them on the album. If it didn't fit the record, I kicked it off!"

Born in New York City and raised by her mother, a sculptor, and her father, a classical composer, Ingrid has artistry in her DNA. At four she began taking piano lessons but it wasn't until after she graduated college with a degree in musical theater and was touring the country in a theater troupe that she began to write the dreamy, pensive-but-poppy songs that would connect with millions. Her music taps into universal themes like self-doubt, betrayal, and, of course, love, but her spirit is fiercely indie; Ingrid's last studio album, 2007's *Girls and Boys*, was released on the label she founded, Cabin 24 Records.

The record's soaring delicacy caught the ear of *Grey's Anatomy*'s music supervisor, and after featuring several of her songs in earlier episodes, Ingrid's heart-wrenching ode to emotional paralysis, "Keep Breathing," was chosen to soundtrack the show's 2007 season finale, which more than 25 million teary-eyed fans watched. Afterwards, everyone went Ingrid crazy: Her lyrics and name were No. 1 and No. 2 on Google's most-searched items list, *Girls and Boys* climbed the iTunes charts, and she began to earn national media attention.

That fall, when Ingrid's song "The Way I Am" was featured in Old Navy's commercial, it propelled *Girls and Boys* into the *Billboard* Top 200 and the record hit No. 1 on both the Heatseeker and Alternative New Artist Album charts. Ingrid's MySpace page registered 90,000 hits per day and she reached the No. 4 song overall on iTunes—all unprecedented feats for an independent release. Since then, Ingrid has continued to chart on the *Billboard* Top 200 multiple times, selling over 300,000 copies of *Girls and Boys*.

Since the release of *Girls and Boys*, Ingrid has appeared on *Good Morning America, Live with Regis and Kelly, Late Night with Conan O'Brien, The Tonight Show with Jay Leno,* NPR's *Talk of the Nation,* Fuse TV, and was a VH1 "You Oughta Know" artist. She has also been the subject of print features in publications as varied as *The Wall Street Journal, The New York Times, The New Yorker, Rolling Stone, Entertainment Weekly,* and *Billboard.*

Ingrid's rise was so quick that she didn't have time to ease into touring. Within a few months the singer, who had never played more than a few local shows at a time, found herself on tour with Dave Matthews and Jason Mraz, and was selling out 1500-capacity club venues on her own. Ingrid adjusted with typical alacrity and good-humor, honing a performance style that's very much in keeping with her quirky personality. Her sets routinely include her now-plentiful list of hits plus witty covers of songs like "Ice Ice Baby" and the theme song from *The Fresh Prince of Bel-Air.*

With all her heady success Ingrid could easily have gone diva by now, but that's not her style. Instead of lounging by a hotel pool demanding bowls of green Jolly Ranchers or falling out of clubs at four in the morning in foreign cities, she amuses herself by making up dances to Jordin Sparks songs with her roommate, then putting them on YouTube. And she keeps herself creatively fresh by insisting on a similar level of commitment to individualism in the way she approaches her work. "I did most of the vocals for the new record at Shelter Island Studios, but I ended up redoing them in my producer's closet, which is his vocal booth," Ingrid says of her work with producer Dan Romer. "I felt better being in there for some reason. [The first single] 'Maybe' wasn't going to be on the record. It was a song we threw together at the last minute and it ended up being the single. The other single, 'Everybody'—we recorded the drums at the fancy studio and sang at the fancy studio, but everything has been redone at Dan's house anyway. When I was in Dan's house there was no pressure."

It's exactly this insistence on keeping things unflinchingly honest, regardless of professional success or personal heartache, that defines Ingrid's connection to her fans. She rose to fame by singing about her faith in love, and now she's written an album that questions that faith, which she knows is risky but also knows is right. "With the first album I was just learning how to use my tools. Now I feel like I can sharpen my skills and say things how I want to say them. Now I feel free to say things about myself that I would have maybe been embarrassed about before. It's like a big old therapy session."

# Soldier

Words and Music by
Ingrid Michaelson

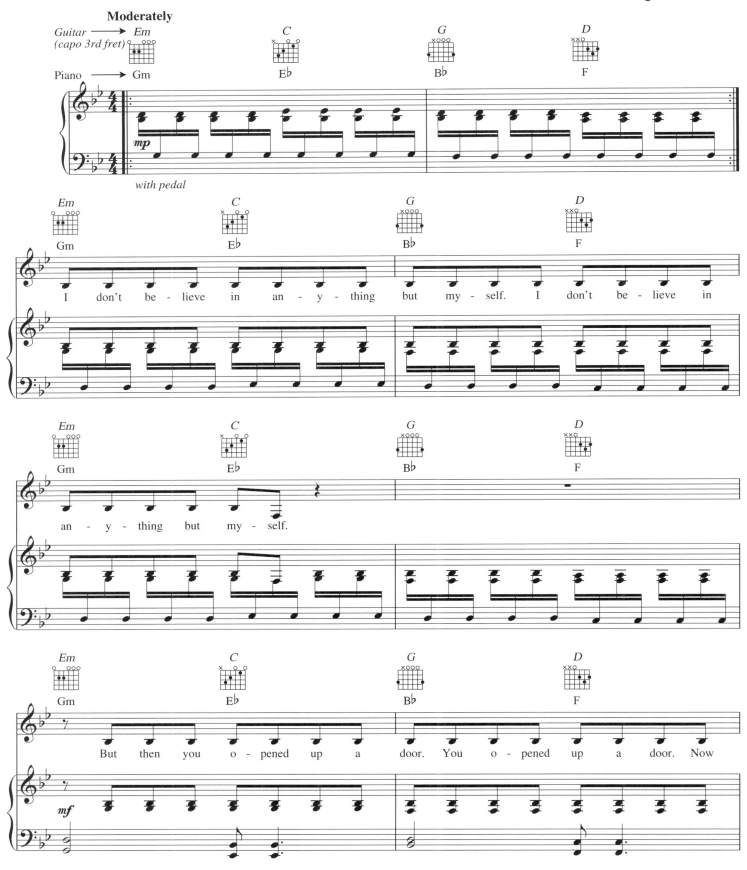

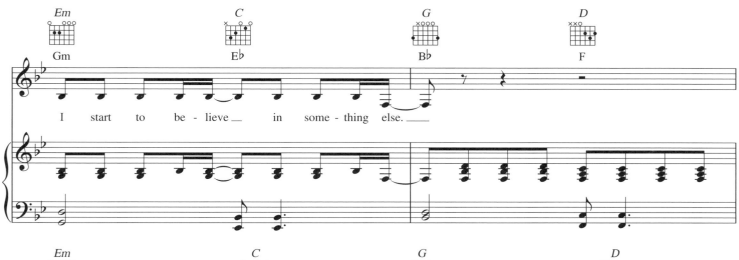

I start to be - lieve __ in some - thing else. __

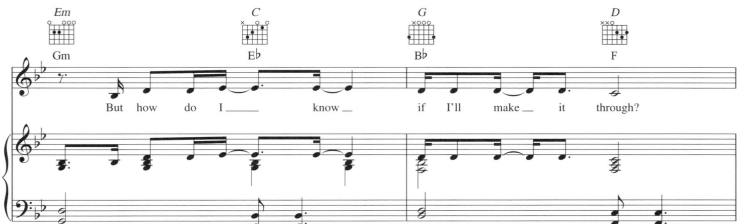

But how do I ___ know __ if I'll make __ it through?

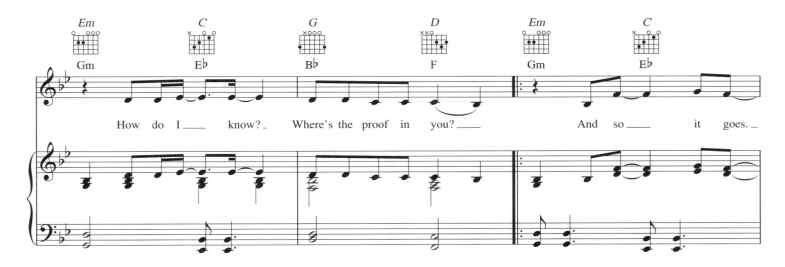

How do I ___ know? _ Where's the proof in you? ___ And so ___ it goes. _

___ This sol - dier knows __ the bat - tle with the heart __ is - n't eas - i - ly won.

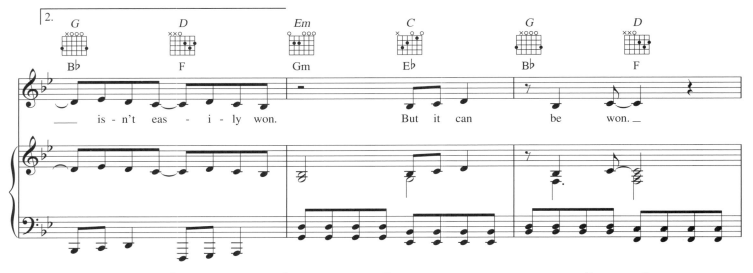

_____ is-n't eas - i - ly won. But it can be won. _____

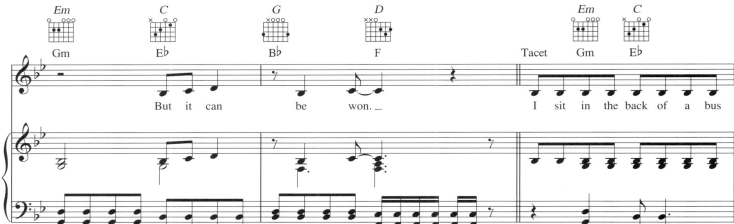

But it can be won. _____ I sit in the back of a bus

watch-ing the world grow old, watch-ing the world go by all by my - self.

I took a faith-ful leap and packed up all my things, and all _____ my love, and gave it to some-bod - y else. _____

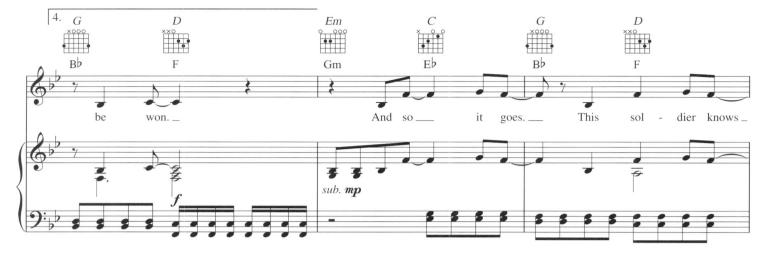

be won. ___ And so ___ it goes. ___ This sol - dier knows ___

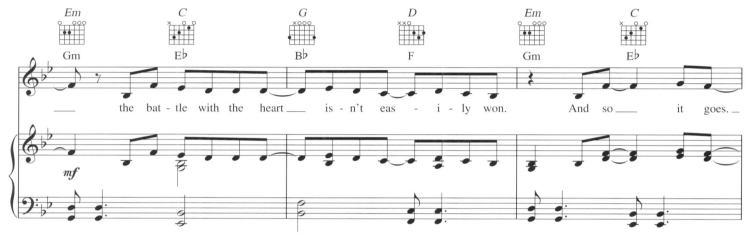

___ the bat - tle with the heart ___ is - n't eas - i - ly won. And so ___ it goes. ___

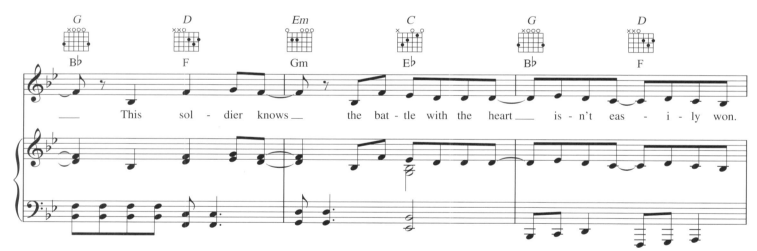

___ This sol - dier knows ___ the bat - tle with the heart ___ is - n't eas - i - ly won.

And so ___ it goes. ___ This sol - dier knows ___ the bat - tle with the heart ___
(And so ___ it goes. ___ The war ___

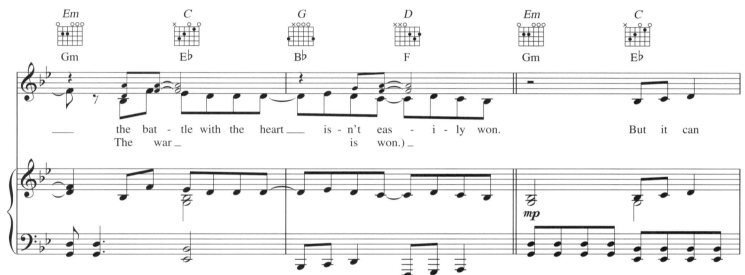

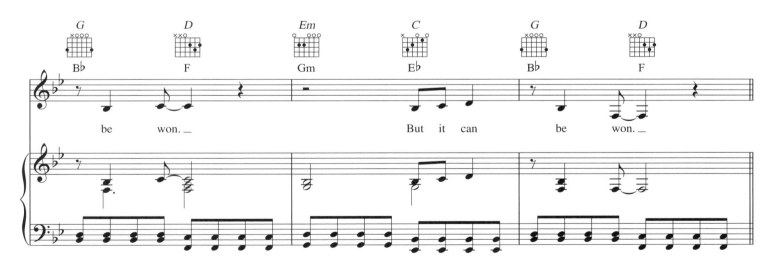

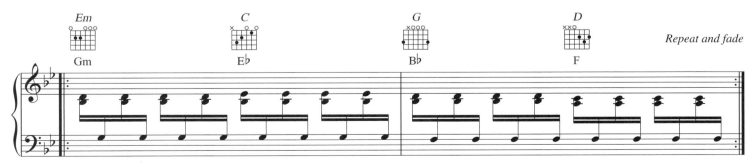

# Everybody

Words and Music by
Ingrid Michaelson

*Recorded a half step lower.
  Guitarists: Capo at 4th fret to play along with recording.

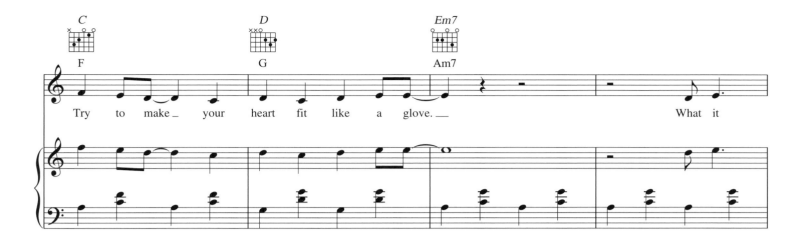

Try to make _ your heart fit like a glove. _ What it

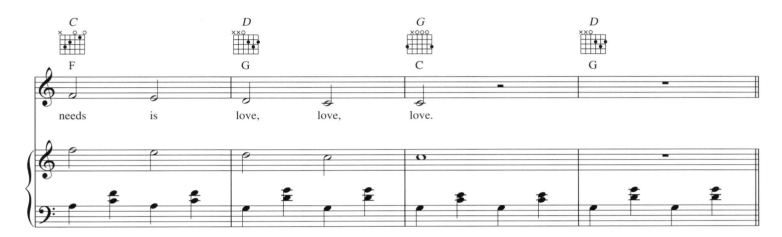

needs is love, love, love.

Ev - 'ry - bod - y, ev - 'ry - bod - y wants to love. _ Ev - 'ry - bod - y, ev - 'ry - bod - y

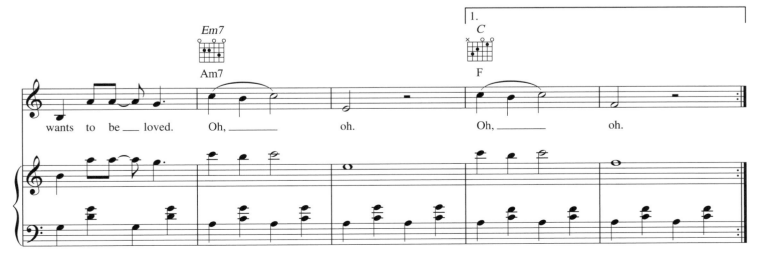

wants to be _ loved. Oh, _____ oh. Oh, _____ oh.

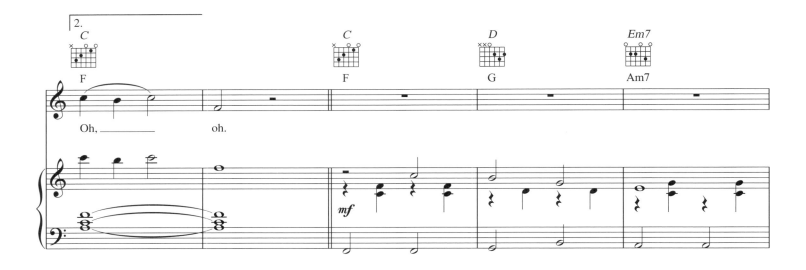

Oh, _____ oh.

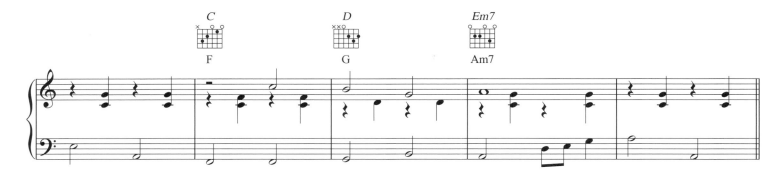

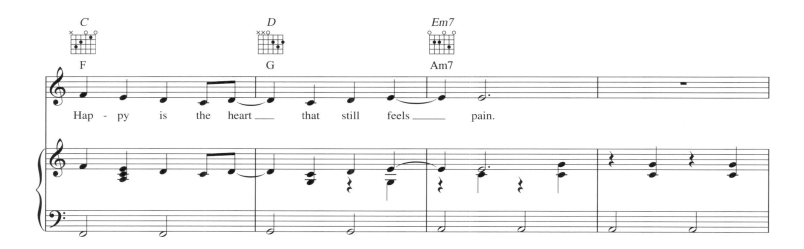

Hap - py is the heart ____ that still feels ____ pain.

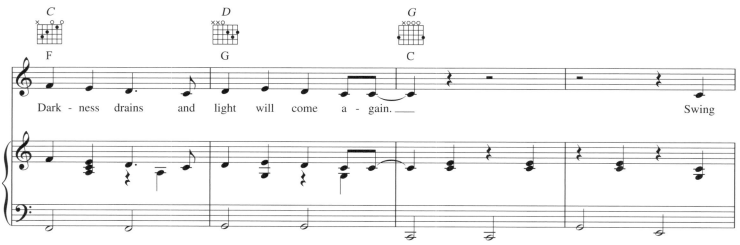

Dark - ness drains and light will come a - gain. ____ Swing

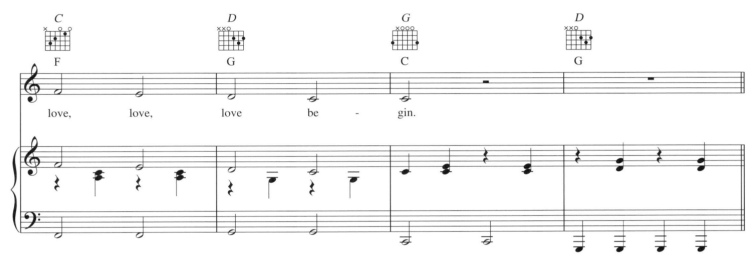

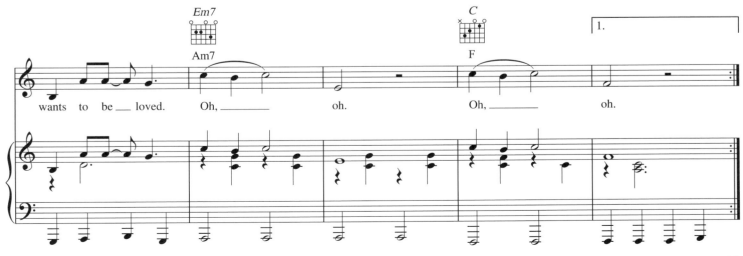

oh. Oh, ev - 'ry - bod - y knows the love. ___ Ev - 'ry - bod - y

holds the love. ___ Ev - 'ry - bod - y folds for love. ___

Ev - 'ry - bod - y feels the love. ___ Ev - 'ry - bod - y

steals the love. ___ Ev - 'ry - bod - y heals with love. ___

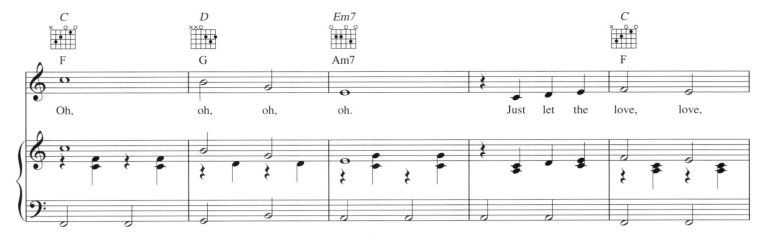

Oh, oh, oh, oh. Just let the love, love,

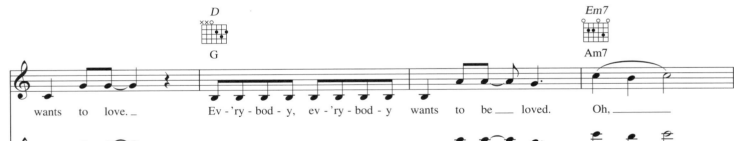

love be - gin. Ev -'ry-bod - y, ev -'ry-bod - y

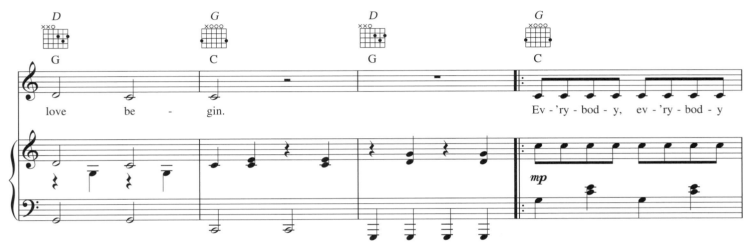

wants to love. _ Ev -'ry-bod - y, ev -'ry-bod - y wants to be __ loved. Oh, _____

1.

2.

oh.
(Just let the love, love, love be - gin.) love, love, love be - gin.)

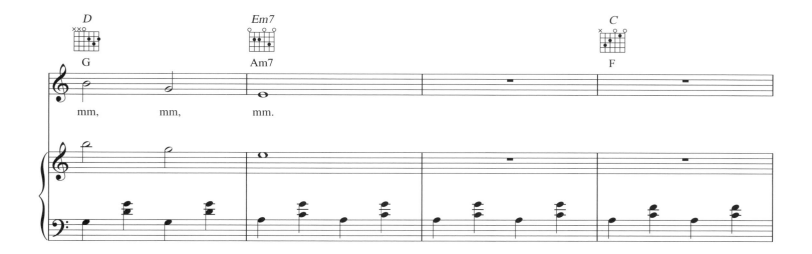

# Are We There Yet

Words and Music by
Ingrid Michaelson

Lyrics:

They say that home __ is where the heart __ is.

I guess __ I have-n't found __ my _____ home.

And we __ keep driv - ing 'round __ in cir - cles, __

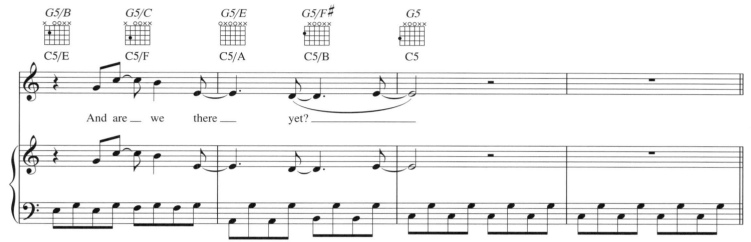

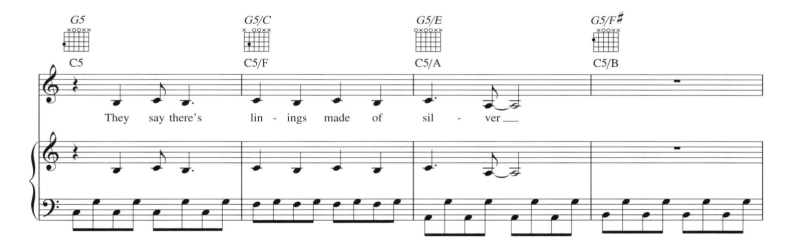

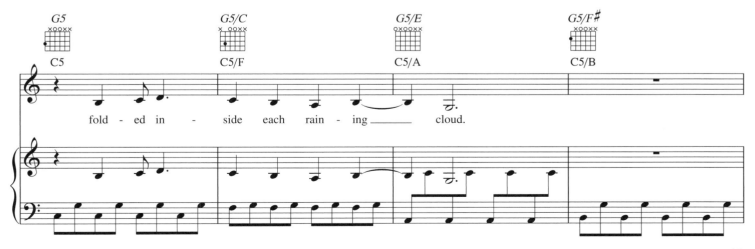

Well, we __ need some - one to __ de - liv - er _____ our __

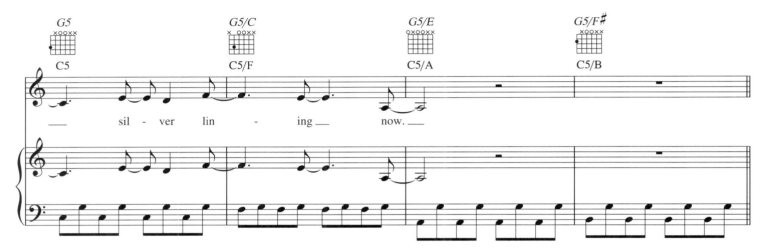

__ sil - ver lin - ing __ now. __

And are __ we there ___ yet? _____ And are __ we there ___ yet? _ And

are we there yet? Home, home, _____ home.

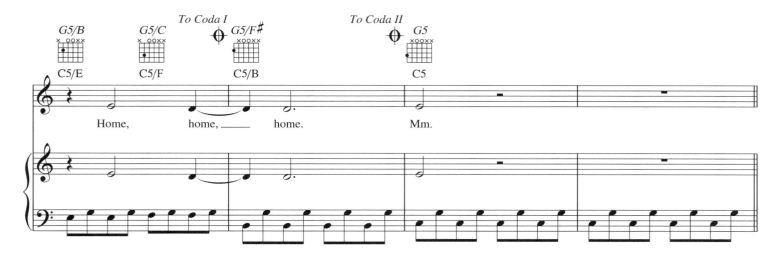

Home, home, _____ home. Mm.

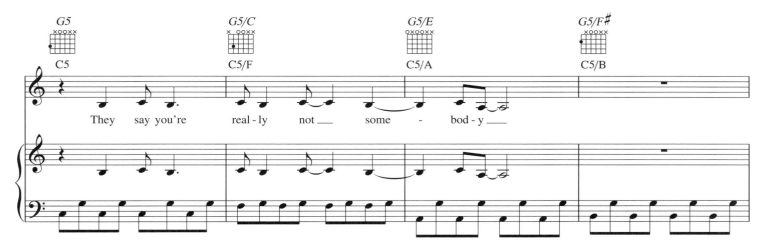

They say you're real-ly not _____ some - bod-y _____

un - til _____ some - bod-y else loves _____ you.

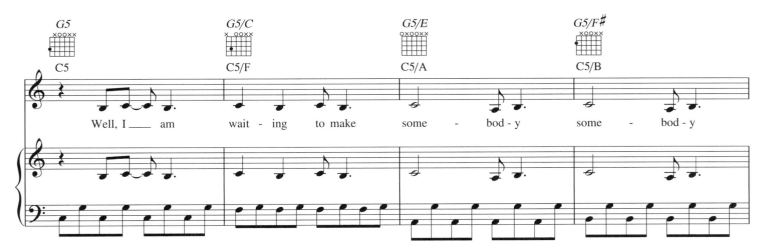

Well, I _____ am wait - ing to make some - bod-y some - bod-y

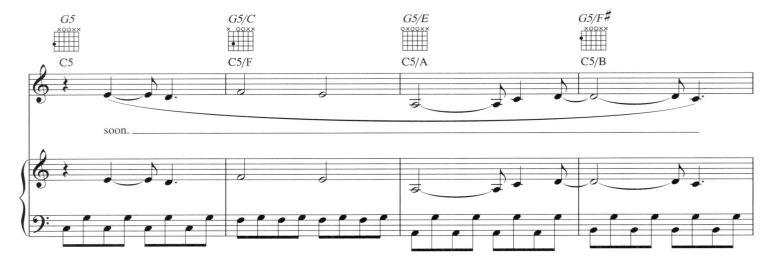

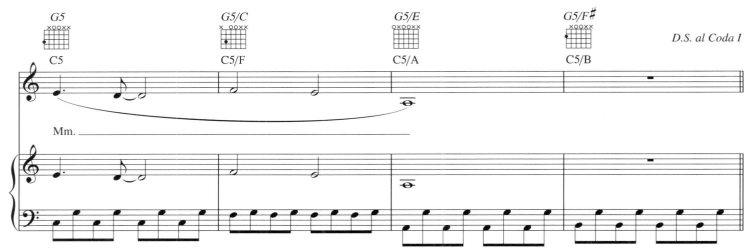

# Sort Of

Words and Music by
Ingrid Michaelson

love's _ too big _ for you, _ my love. _

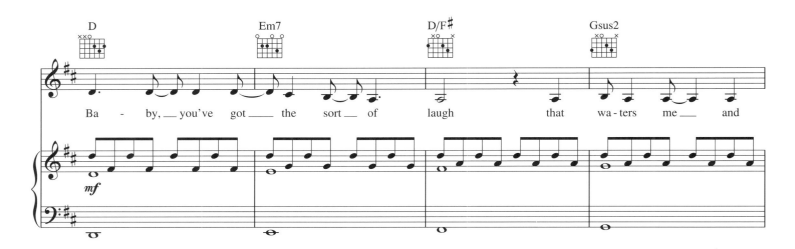

Ba - by, _ you've got _ the sort _ of laugh that wa - ters me _ and

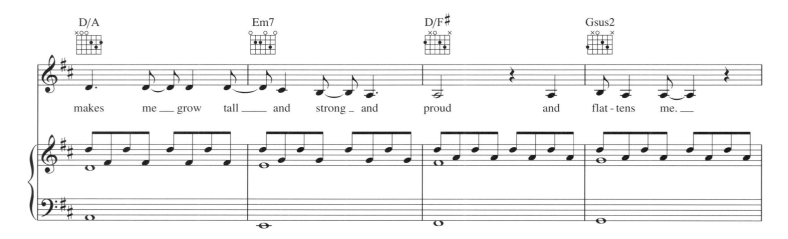

makes me _ grow tall _ and strong _ and proud and flat - tens me. _

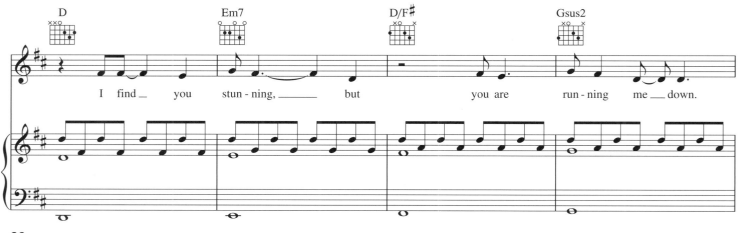

I find _ you stun - ning, _____ but you are run - ning me _ down.

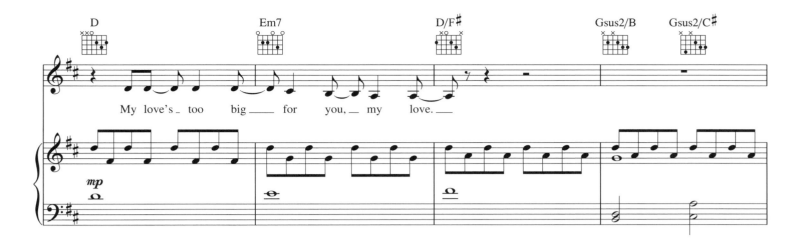

My love's _ too  big ___ for  you, _  my  love. __

My love's _ too  big ___ for  you, _  my  love. __                                                                And

if   I ___ was   strong - er, _____ then  I _____                     would tell ___   you _ no.  And

if   I ___ was   strong - er, _____ then  I _____                     will leave _   this _ show.  And

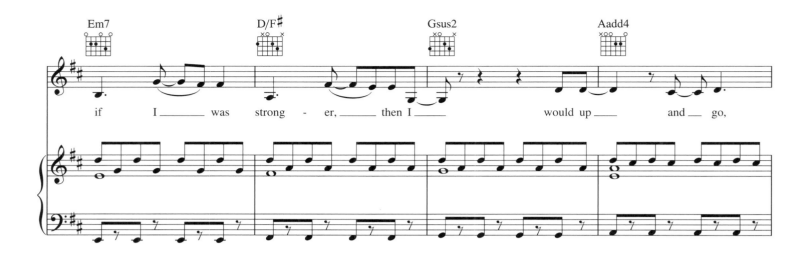

if I _____ was strong - er, _____ then I _____ would up _____ and __ go,

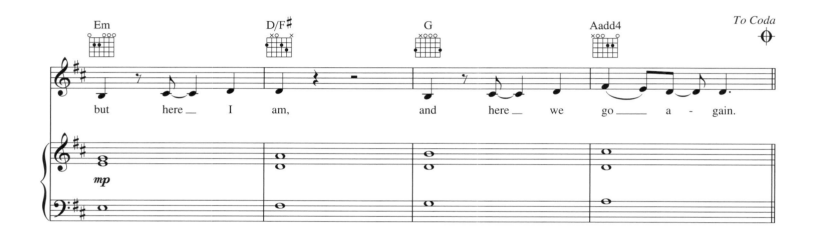

but here __ I am, and here __ we go _____ a - gain.

*To Coda* ⊕

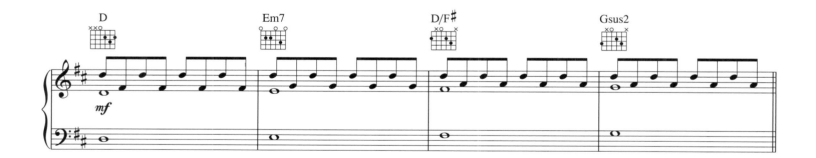

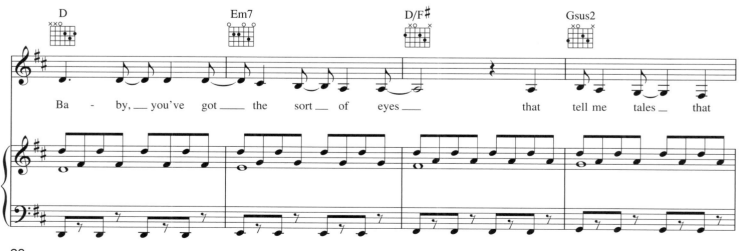

Ba - by, __ you've got __ the sort __ of eyes _____ that tell me tales __ that

28

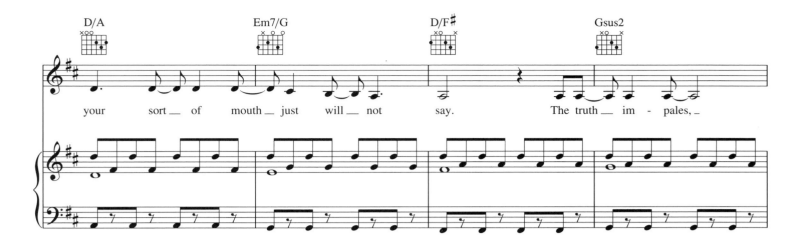

your sort __ of mouth __ just will __ not say. The truth __ im - pales, __

that you __ don't need me, __ but you __ won't leave me. __

My love's __ too big __ for you, __ my love. __ Oh. _____

*D.S. al Coda*

My love's __ too big __ for you, __ my love. __ And

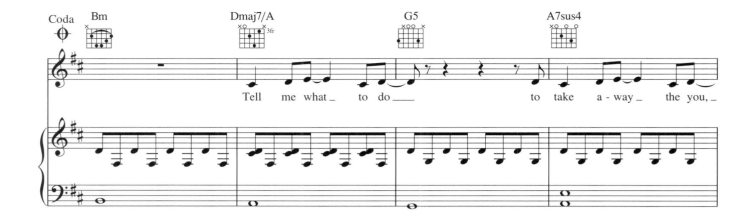

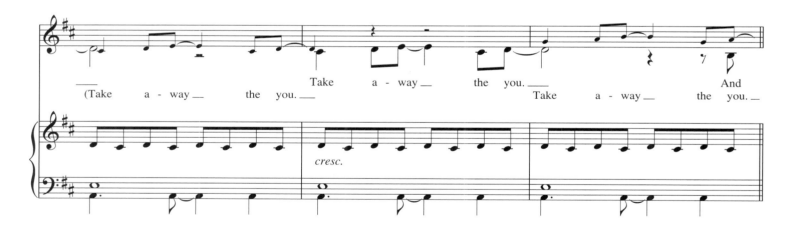

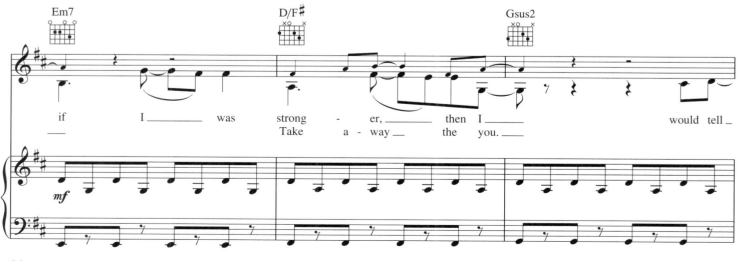

Take a- way ___ the you. ___ you ___ no. And if I ___ was strong - er, ___ then I ___

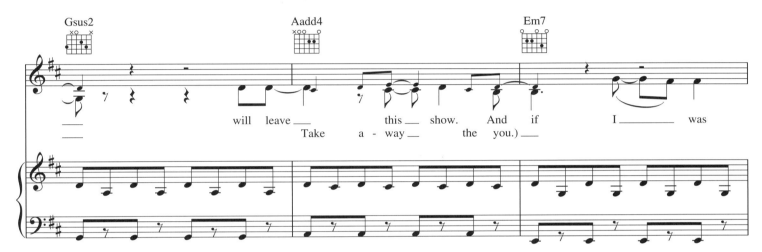

___ will leave ___ this ___ show. And if I ___ was
Take a- way ___ the you.) ___

strong - er, ___ then I ___ would up ___ and ___ go,

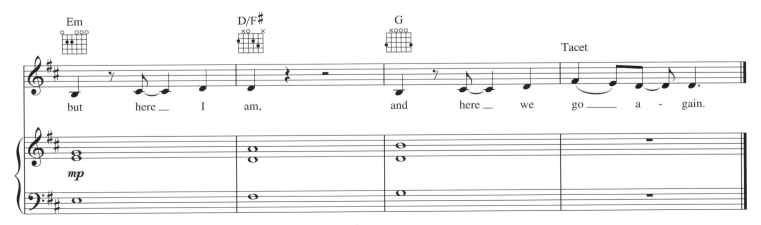

but here ___ I am, and here ___ we go ___ a- gain.

31

# Incredible Love

Words and Music by
Ingrid Michaelson

would give me more _____ room _____ to breathe. _

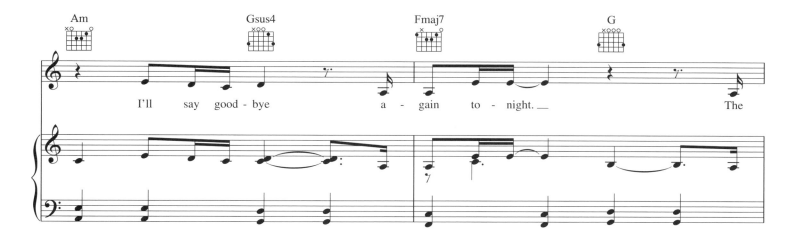

I'll say good-bye a - gain to - night. __ The

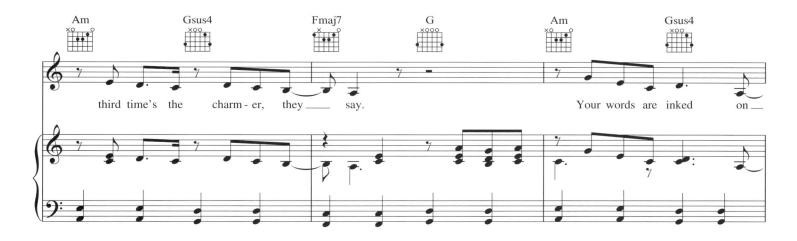

third time's the charm - er, they _____ say. Your words are inked on _

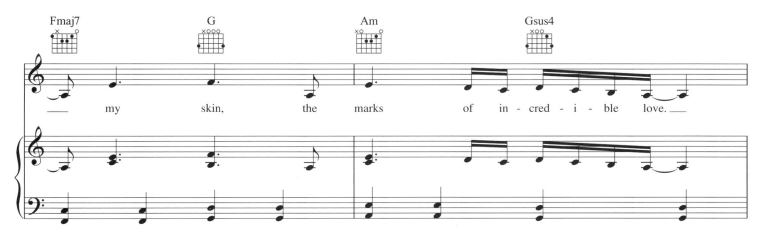

_ my skin, the marks of in - cred - i - ble love. _

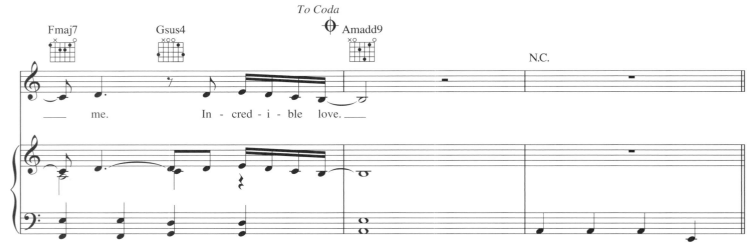

34

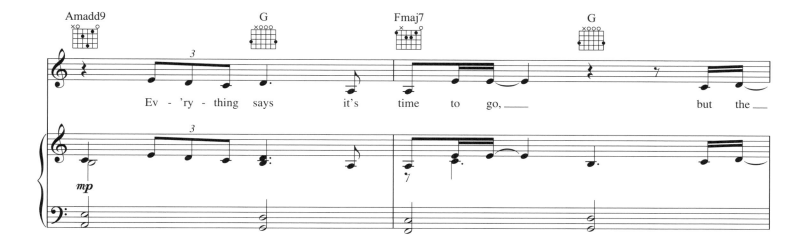

Ev - 'ry - thing says it's time to go, _____ but the _____

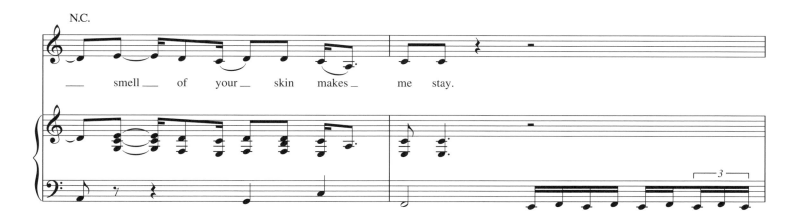

_____ smell _____ of your _____ skin makes _____ me stay.

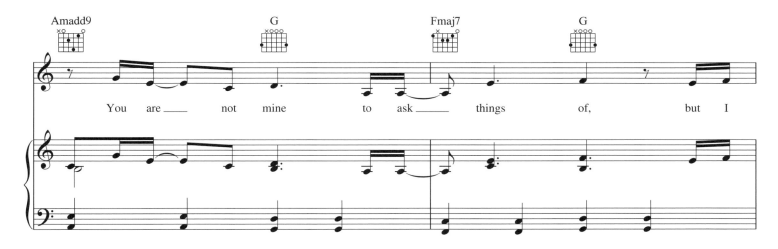

You are _____ not mine to ask _____ things of, but I

*D.S. al Coda*

ask you an - y - way, I ask you an - y - way. _____ In -

back. ___ Don't give it back. _____ (In - cred - i - ble love, ___ in - cred - i - ble love, ___

___ in - cred - i - ble love. ___ In - cred - i - ble love, ___ in - cred - i - ble love, ___

___ in - cred - i - ble love.) ___ In - cred - i - ble love, ___ you fill ___

___ me. _____
(In - cred - i - ble love, ___ you fill _____ me.
In - cred - i - ble love, ___ you spill ___

me.
In - cred - i - ble love,___ you spill ___ me.

In - cred - i - ble love,___ you kill ___
...kill ___

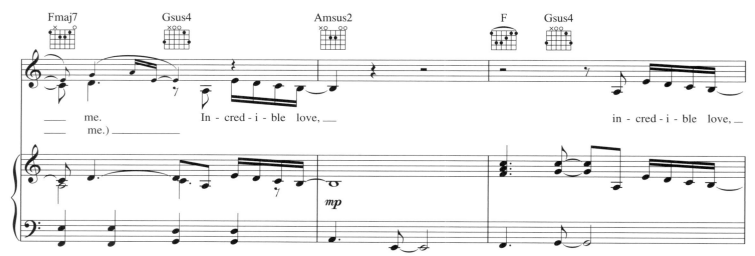

___ me.
In - cred - i - ble love,___
in - cred - i - ble love,___

___ me.)

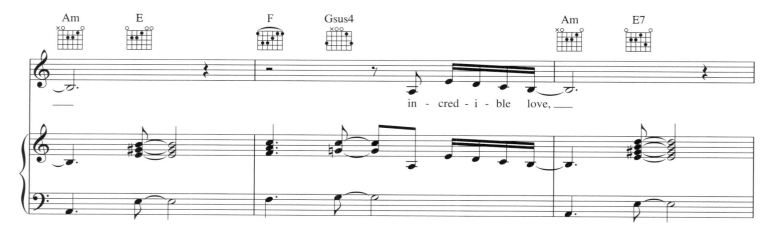

in - cred - i - ble love, ___

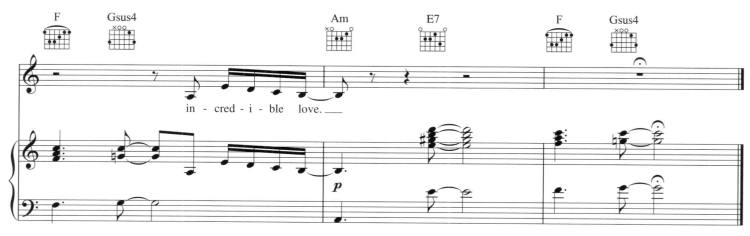

in - cred - i - ble love. ___

# The Chain

Words and Music by
Ingrid Michaelson

**Moderately slow, in 2**

Mm,    mm,    mm,    mm,    mm,    mm,

mm.

The sky    looks ___ pissed;
My room    feels ___ wrong;
I'll nev - er ___ say

*Guitarists: Pluck chords with fingers.

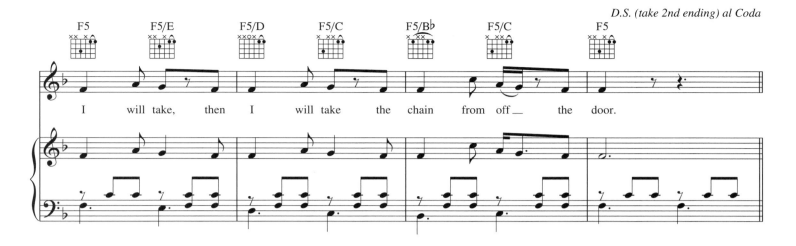

I will take, then I will take the chain from off __ the door.

I will take the chain from off the door. So glide a - way on

\*From here till four measures from end, sing as a round,
with additional voices entering one measure apart.

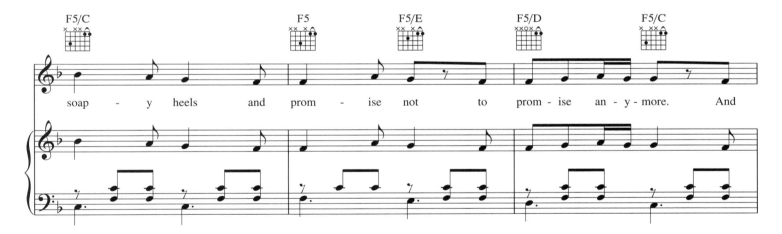

soap - y heels and prom - ise not to prom - ise an - y - more. And

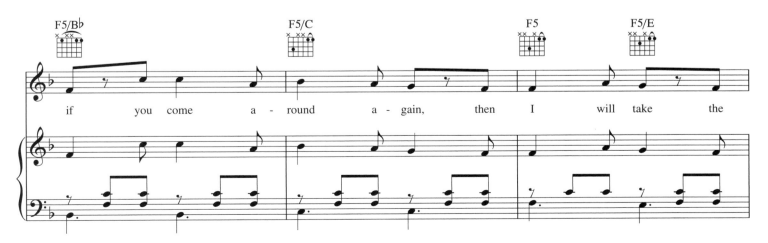

if you come a - round a - gain, then I will take the

41

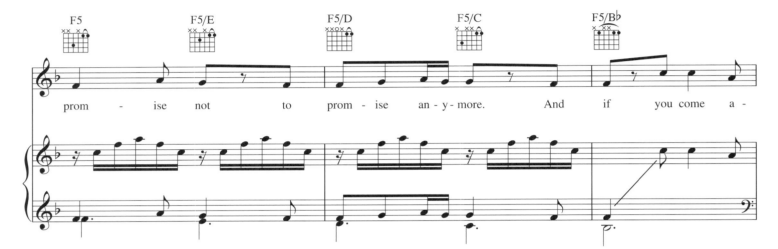

# Mountain and the Sea

Words and Music by
Ingrid Michaelson

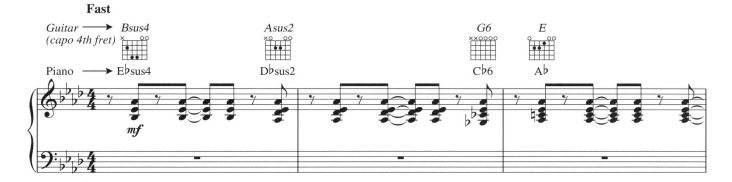

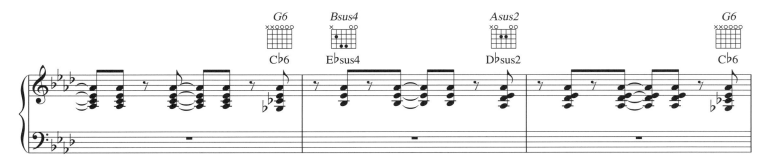

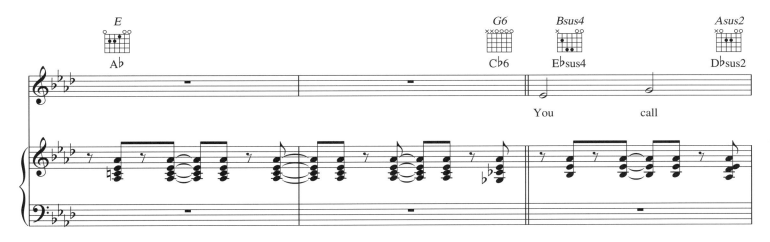

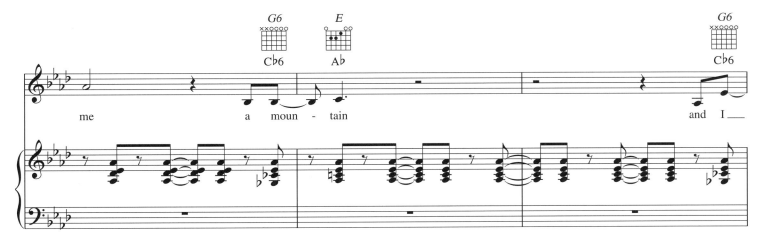

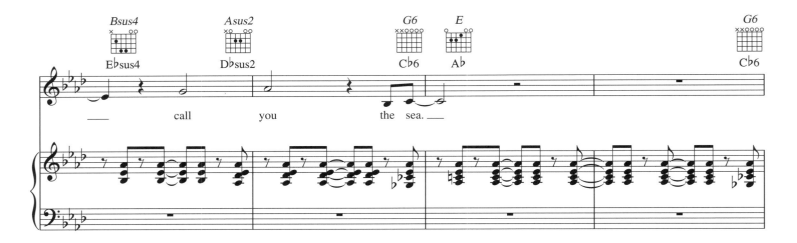

_call you_ _the sea._

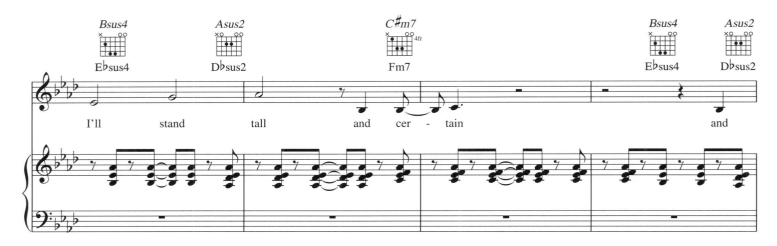

_I'll_ _stand_ _tall_ _and_ _cer - tain_ _and_

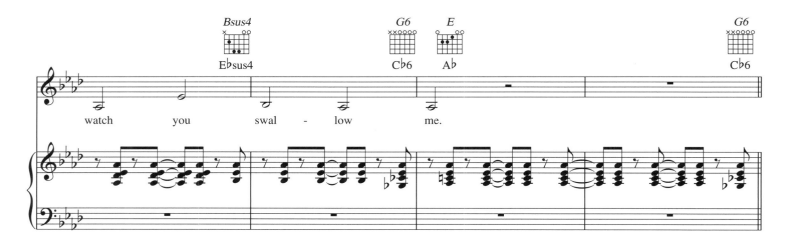

_watch_ _you_ _swal - low_ _me._

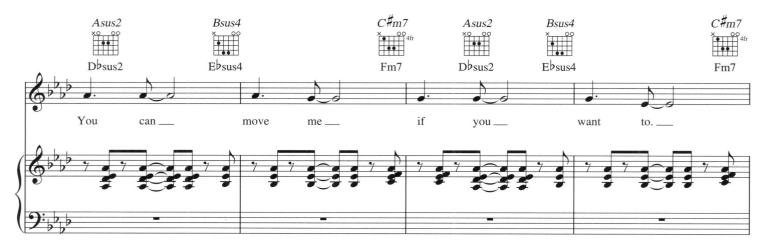

_You_ _can_ _move_ _me_ _if_ _you_ _want_ _to._

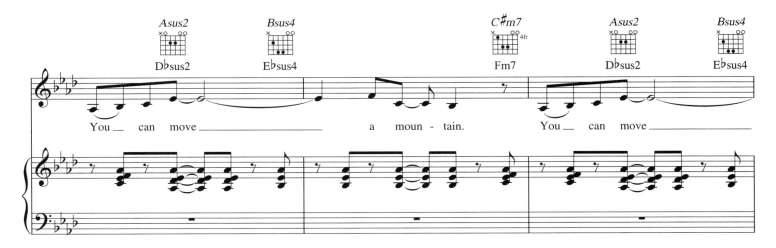

You ___ can move _____ a moun - tain. You ___ can move _____

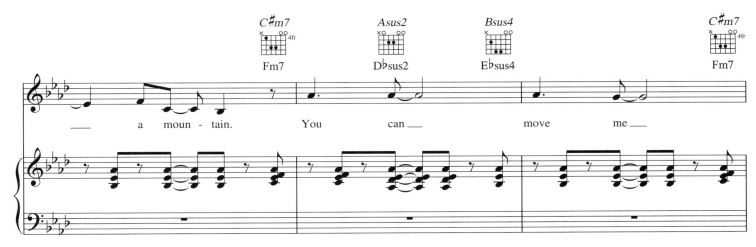

___ a moun - tain. You can ___ move me ___

if you ___ want to. ___ You can move _____

___ ev - 'ry - thing. You ___ can move _____ ev - 'ry - thing.

But then\_\_ one day\_\_ you'll go\_\_ a - way,\_\_ but I\_\_ will too. \_\_ But un - til then, \_\_

oh, my dar - ling friend, \_ well, I \_\_ will \_ hold, \_\_

yes, I \_\_ will will hold, \_\_ yes, I \_\_ will \_ hold, \_\_

# Men of Snow

Words and Music by
Ingrid Michaelson

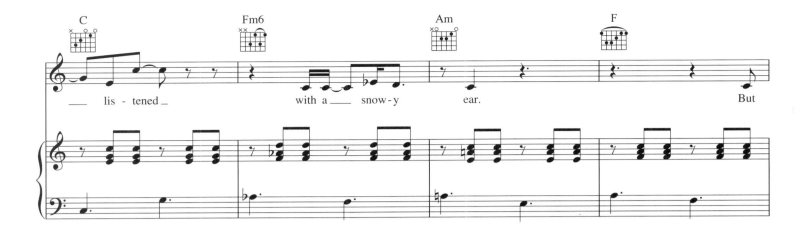

_____ lis - tened _____ with a _____ snow - y ear. But

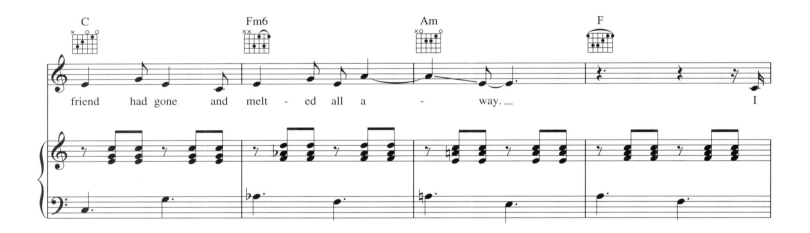

when I came a - round the next day, my

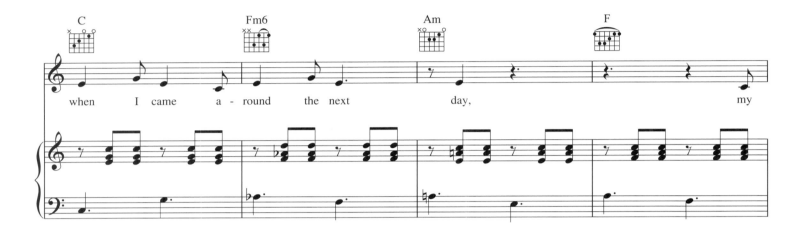

friend had gone and melt - ed all a - way. _____ I

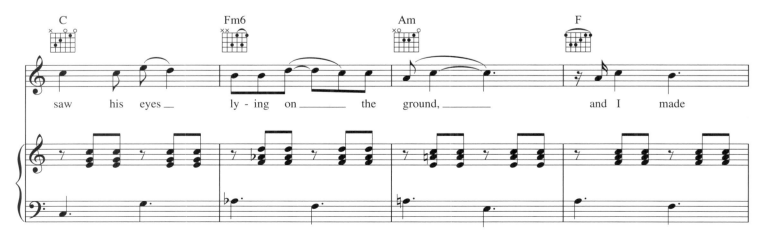

saw his eyes _____ ly - ing on _____ the ground, _____ and I made

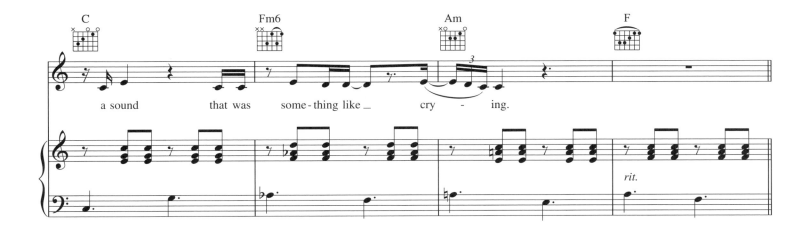

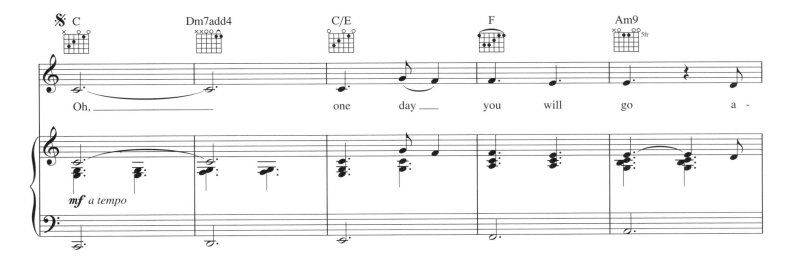

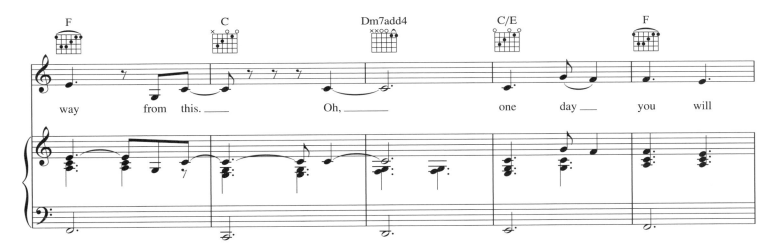

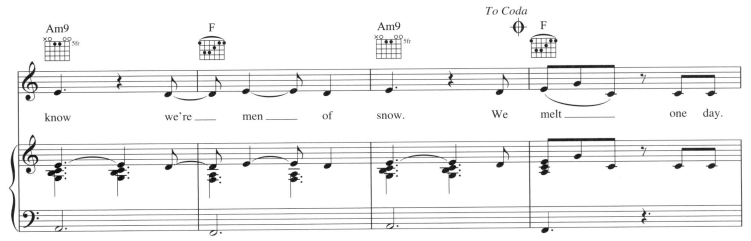

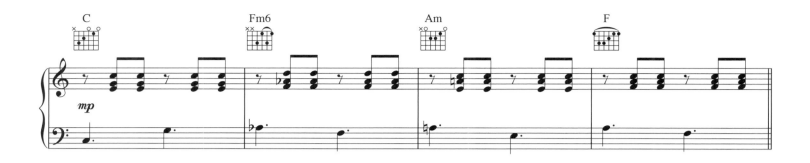

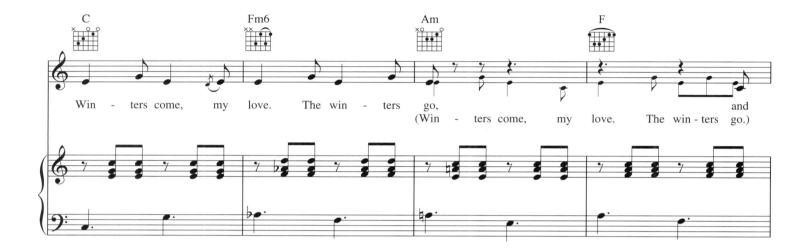

Win - ters come, my love. The win - ters go, and
(Win - ters come, my love. The win - ters go.)

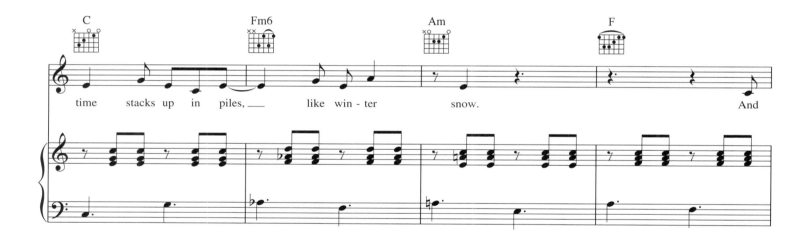

time stacks up in piles, ___ like win - ter snow. And

ev - 'ry - thing you love and hold so ___ dear, ___ it won't ___ real - ly

mat - ter        when we dis - ap - pear. ___

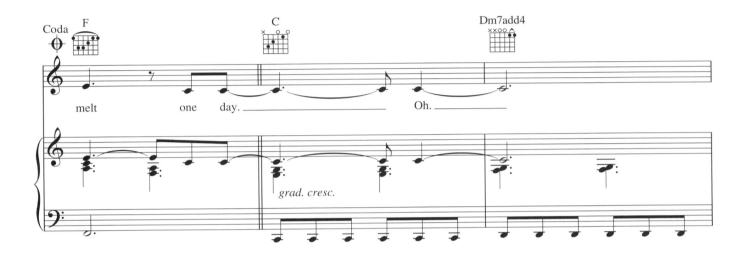

melt        one day. _____ Oh. _____

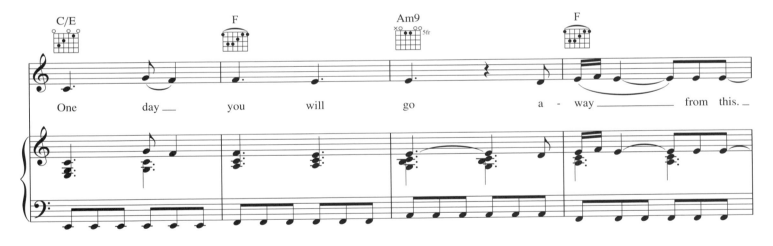

One        day ___ you        will        go        a - way _____ from this. __

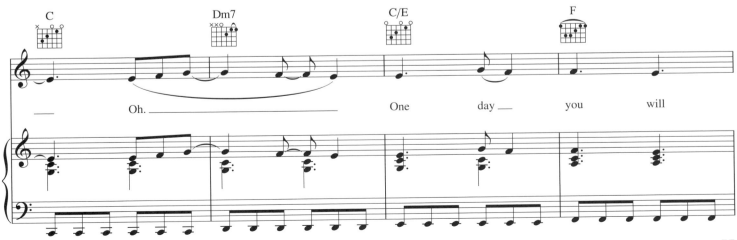

___        Oh. _____        One        day ___ you        will

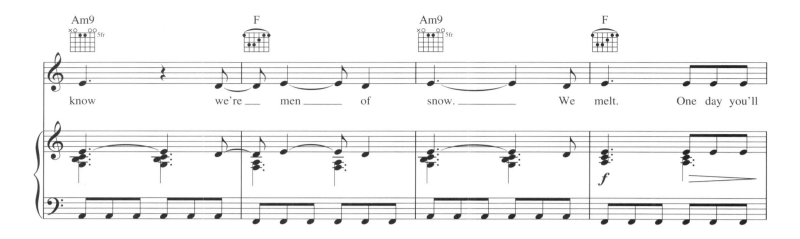

know we're __ men __ of snow. __ We melt. One day you'll

know __ we're men __ of snow. _ We melt __ one day.

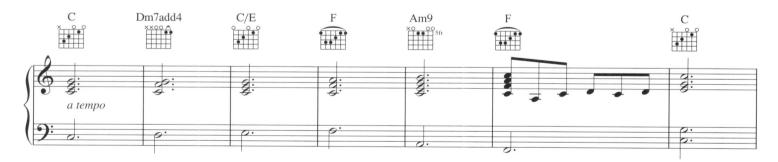

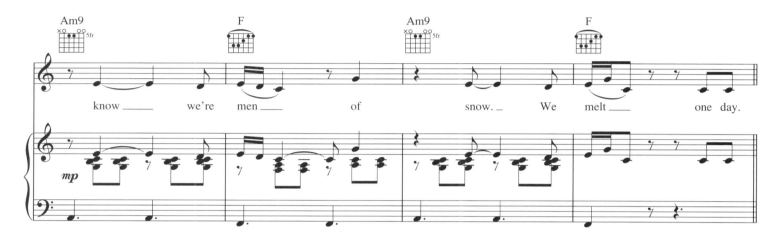

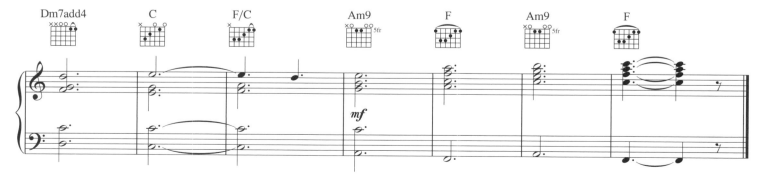

# So Long

Words and Music by
Ingrid Michaelson

*Recorded a half step higher.
Guitarists: Capo at 6th fret to play along with recording.

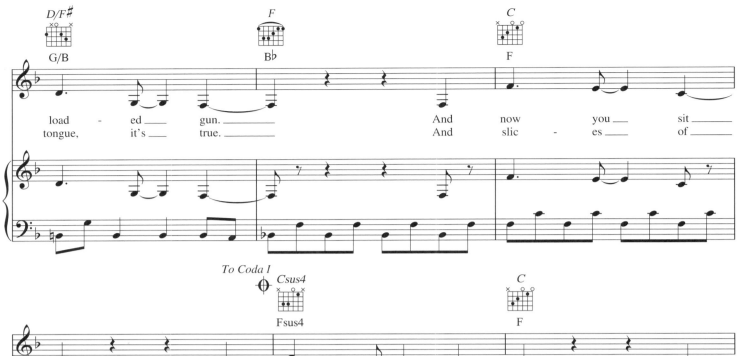

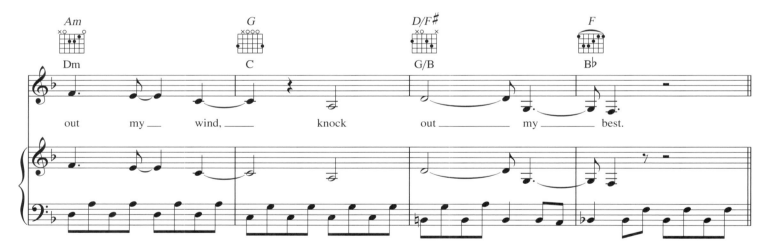

ters _____ and morn - ings, __ too.

And so _____ long _

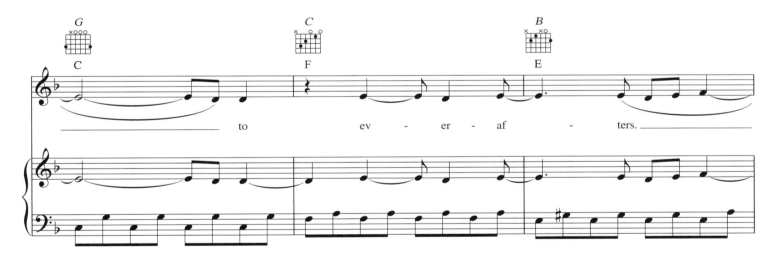

_____ to ev - er - af - ters. _____

*To Coda III*    *To Coda II*    *D.C. al Coda I*

So _____ long _ to you.

piled sky high. ___ The same old ___ me ___

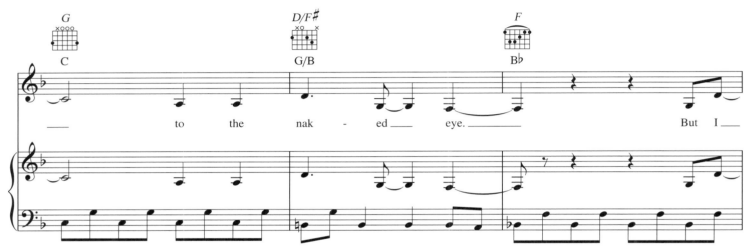

___ to the nak - ed ___ eye. ___ But I ___

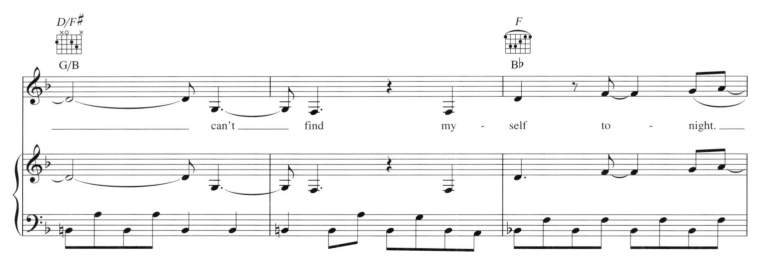

___ can't ___ find my - self to - night. ___

*D.S. al Coda II*

Coda II

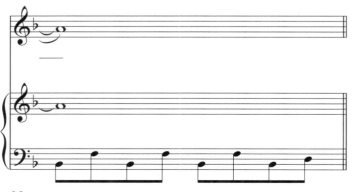

___

to you.

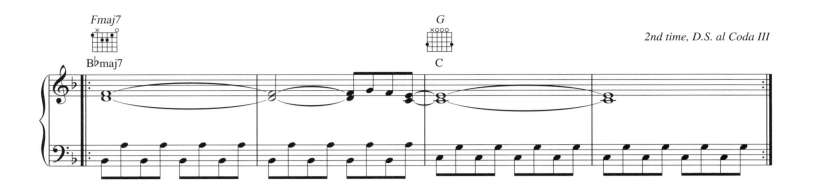

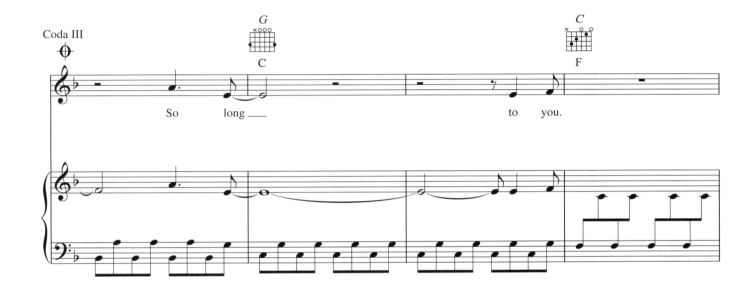

So    long ___                         to    you.

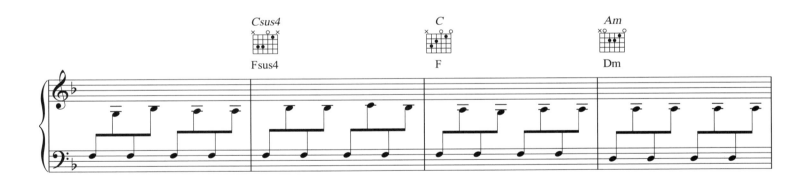

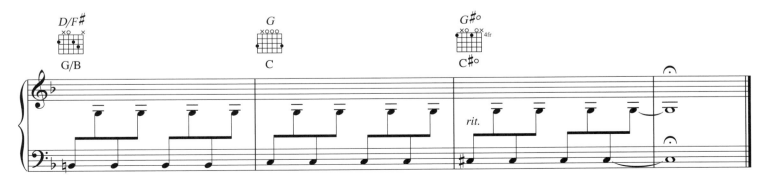

*rit.*

# Once Was Love

Words and Music by
Ingrid Michaelson

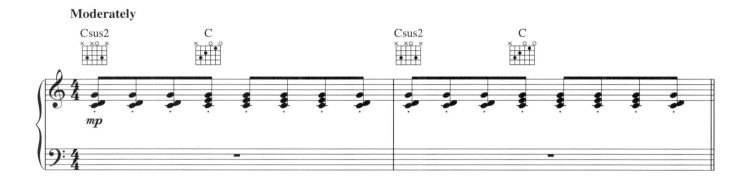

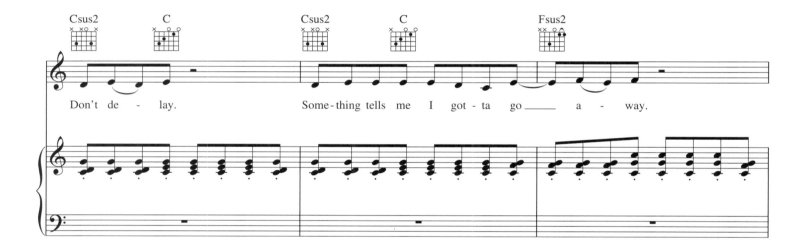

Don't de - lay. Some - thing tells me I got - ta go _____ a - way.

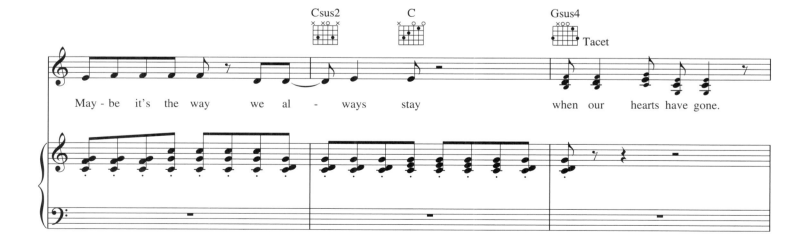

May - be it's the way we al - ways stay when our hearts have gone.

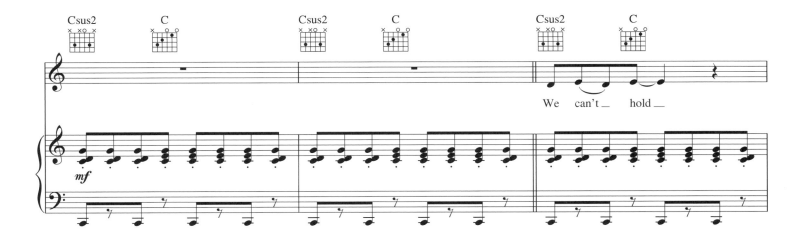

We can't __ hold __

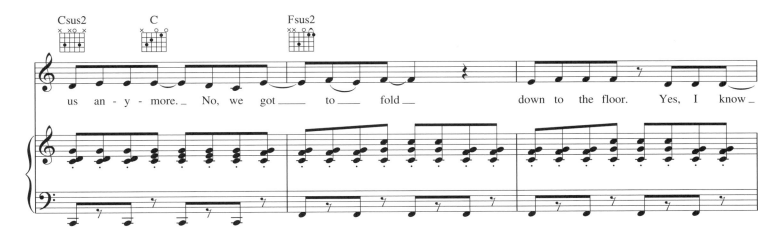

us an - y - more. __ No, we got ____ to __ fold __ down to the floor. Yes, I know __

__ it's cold, __ but, ba - by, our hearts have gone.

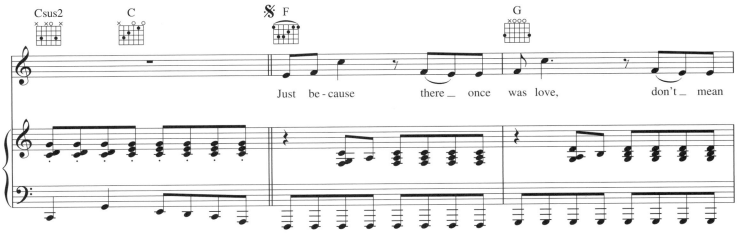

Just be - cause there __ once was love, don't __ mean

a thing, __ don't __ mean a thing, _____ no. Just be - cause there __ once

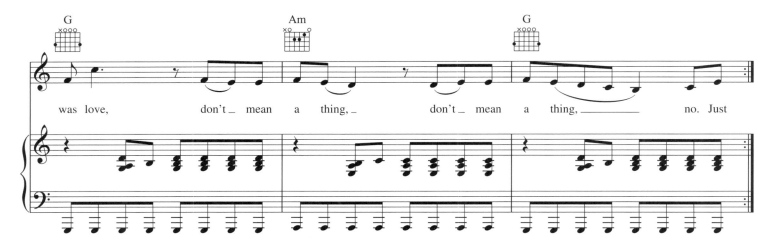

was love, don't __ mean a thing, __ don't __ mean a thing, _____ no. Just

*To Coda* ⊕

be - cause there __ once was love, _____ oh, oh.

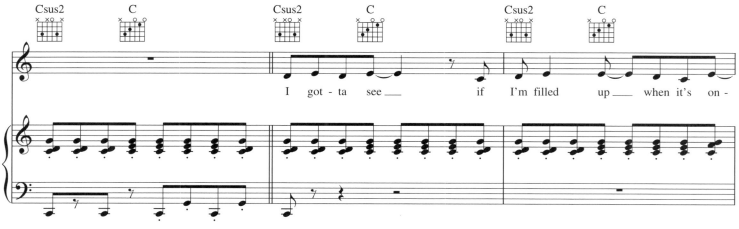

I got - ta see ___ if I'm filled up ___ when it's on -

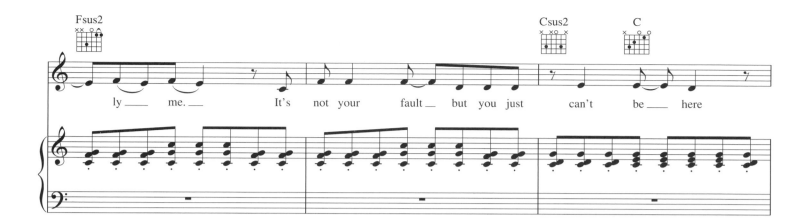

ly \_\_\_\_ me. \_\_\_\_ It's not your fault \_\_\_\_ but you just can't be \_\_\_\_ here

*D.S. (with repeat) al Coda*

now that my heart has gone,     now that my heart has gone,     now that my heart has gone.

was love. _____

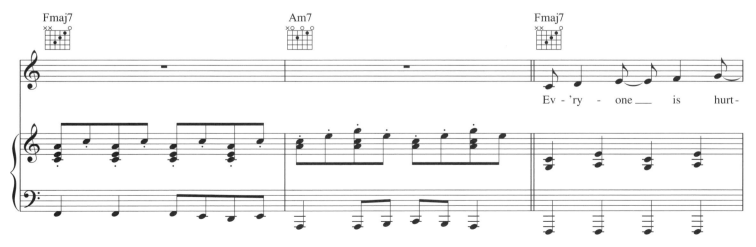

Ev - 'ry - one \_\_\_ is hurt -

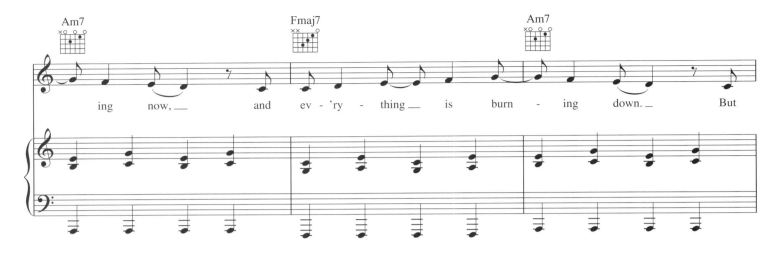

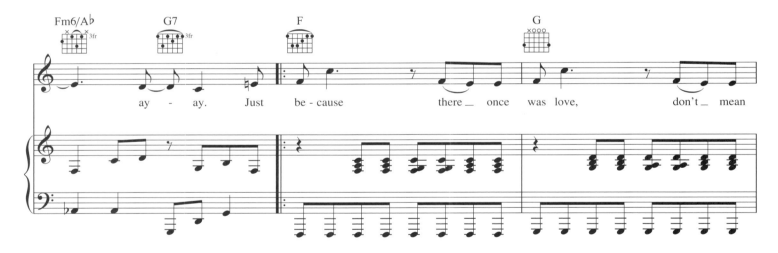

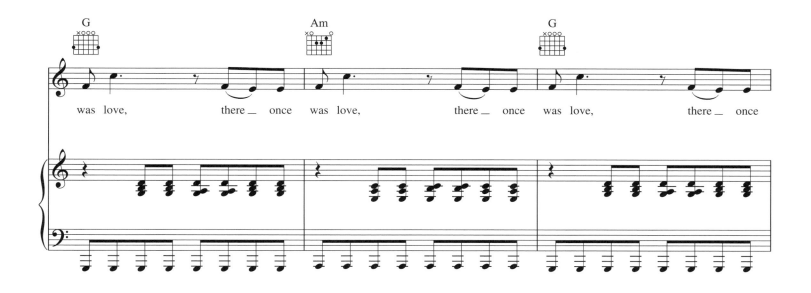

was love,     there __ once was love,     there __ once was love,     there __ once

was     love, __ there __ once was     love, __ there __ once was     love, __ there __ once

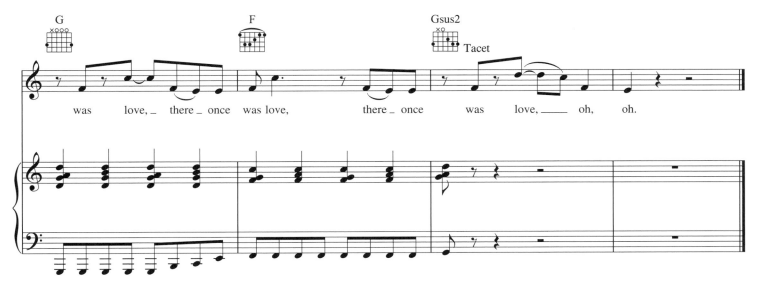

was     love, __ there __ once was love,     there __ once was love, _____ oh,    oh.

# Locked Up

Words and Music by
Ingrid Michaelson

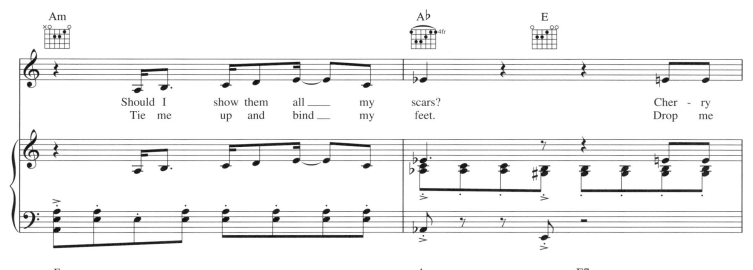

Should I show them all ___ my scars?
Tie me up and bind ___ my feet.

Cher - ry
Drop me

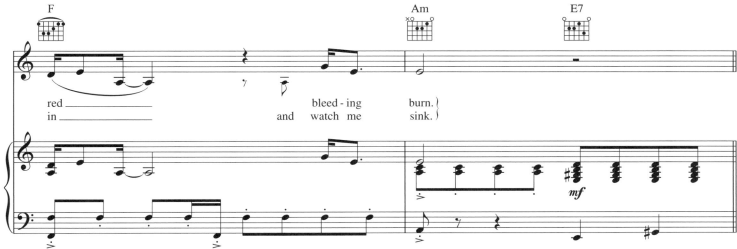

red ___ bleed - ing burn.
in ___ and watch me sink.

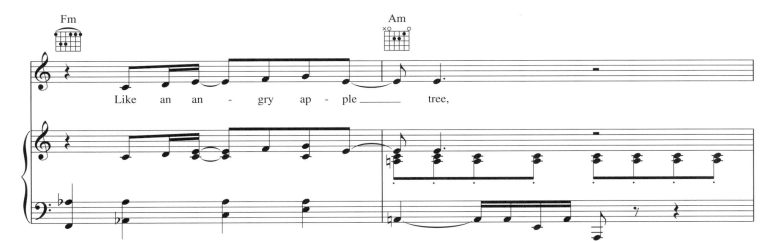

Like an an - gry ap - ple ___ tree,

I throw my ap - ples ___ if you get ___ too close to me. ___

69

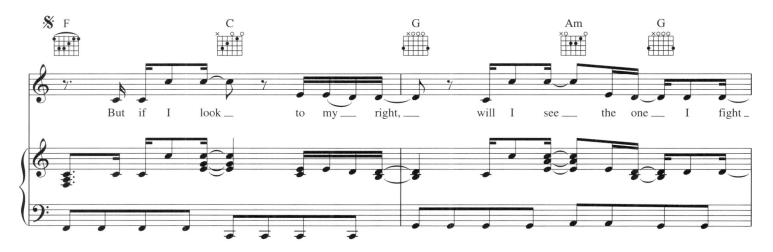

But if I look \_\_ to my \_\_ right, \_\_ will I see \_\_ the one \_\_ I fight \_\_

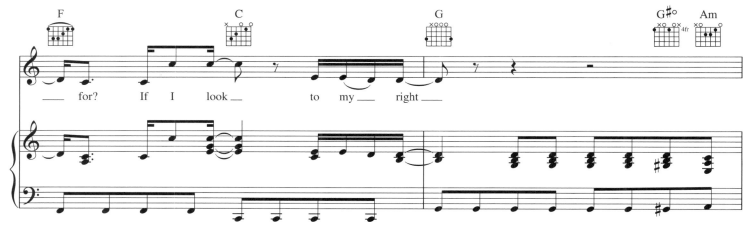

\_\_ for? If I look \_\_ to my \_\_ right \_\_

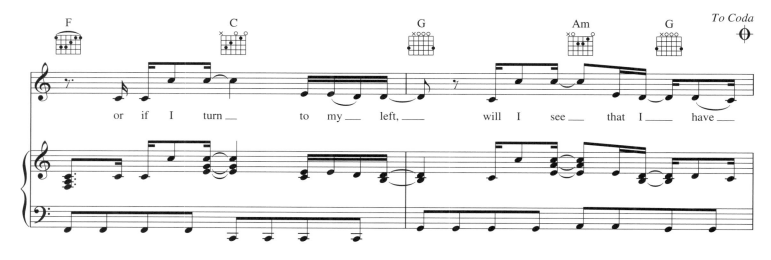

*To Coda*

or if I turn \_\_ to my \_\_ left, \_\_ will I see \_\_ that I \_\_ have \_\_

1.

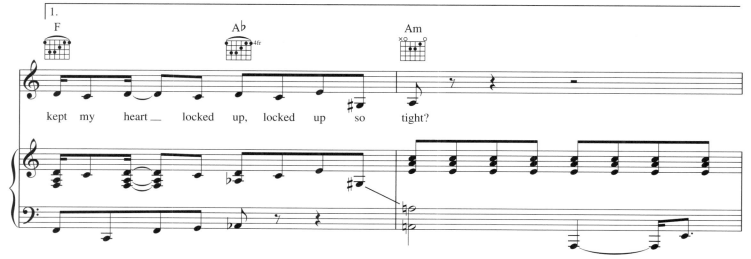

kept my heart \_\_ locked up, locked up so tight?

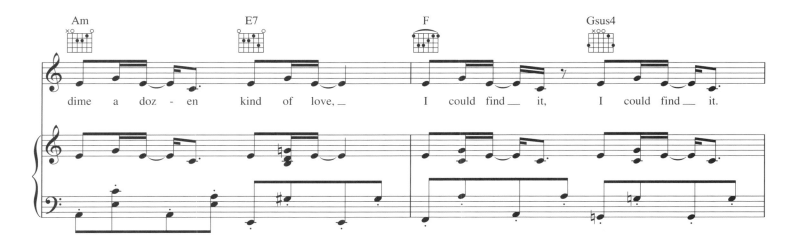

dime a doz - en kind of love, __ I could find __ it, I could find __ it.

But I'm not _____ sev - en - teen _____ and I lost __ it in be - tween _ the birth-

day cakes and fast mis - takes that roll _____ by. __

Ba da bum __ ba da da bum ___ ba da da ba ba da da da ba dum.

Ba da bum __ ba da da bum __ ba da da ba ba da da da ba dum.

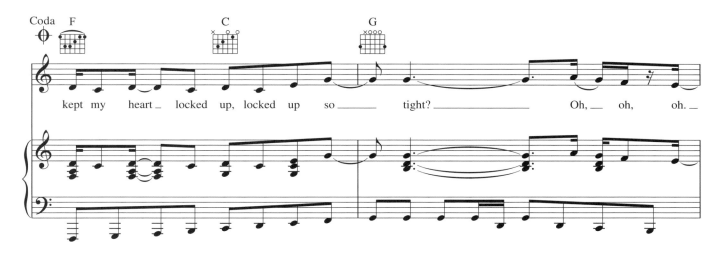

kept my heart __ locked up, locked up so __ tight? __ Oh, __ oh, oh. __

__ Ba da bum __ ba da da bum __ ba da da ba ba da da da ba dum.

Ba da bum __ ba da da bum __ ba da da ba ba da da da ba dum.

Ba da bum ___ ba da da bum ___ ba da da ba ba da da da ba dum.

Ba da bum ___ ba da da bum ___ ba da da ba ba da da da ba dum.

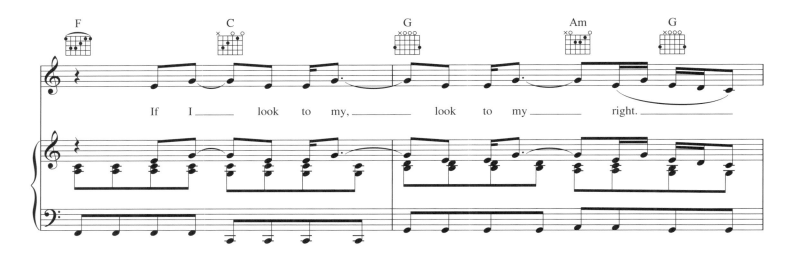

If I ___ look to my, ___ look to my ___ right. ___

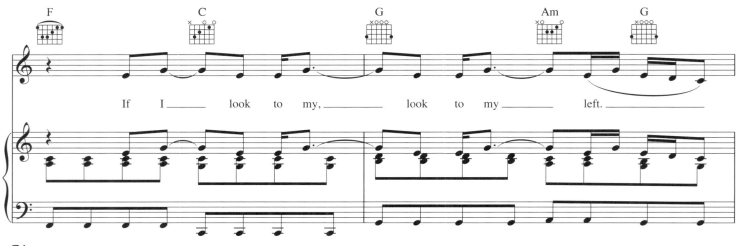

If I ___ look to my, ___ look to my ___ left. ___

If I _____ look to my, _____ look to my right. _____

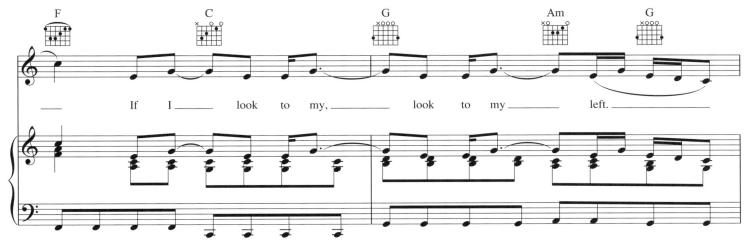

_____ If I _____ look to my, _____ look to my _____ left. _____

If I _____ look to my, _____ look to my right, _ look to my right. _

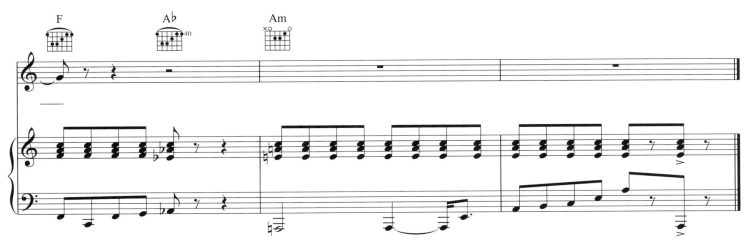

# Maybe

Words and Music by
Ingrid Michaelson

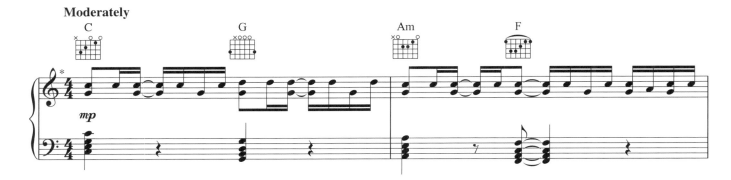

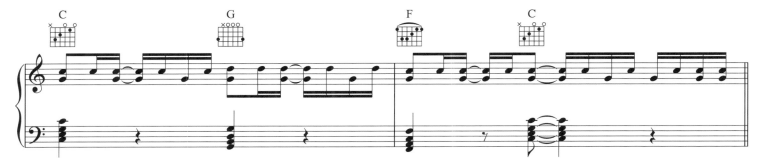

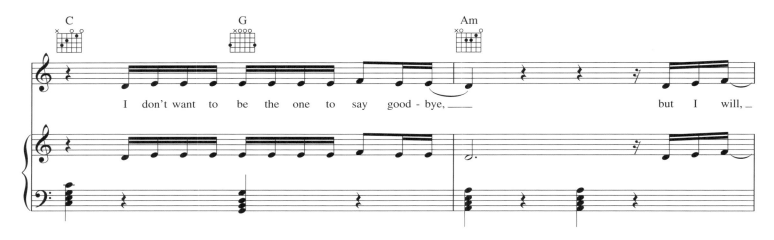

I don't want to be the one to say good - bye, ____ but I will, ____

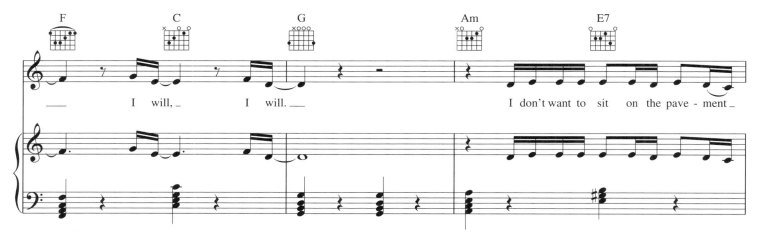

____ I will, ____ I will. ____ I don't want to sit on the pave - ment ____

*Recorded a half step higher.

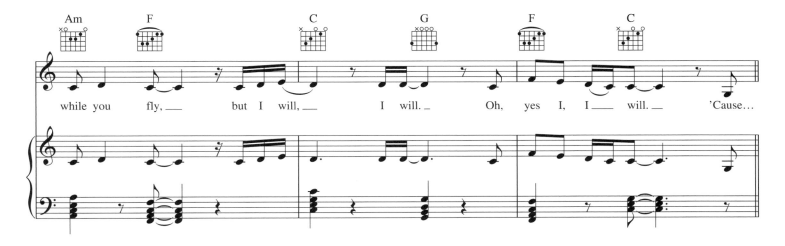

while you fly, ___ but I will, ___ I will. ___ Oh, yes I, I ___ will. ___ 'Cause…

May - be in the fu - ture, you're gon - na come back, you're gon - na come back a - round.

May - be in the fu - ture, you're gon - na come back, you're gon - na come back. Oh, the on -

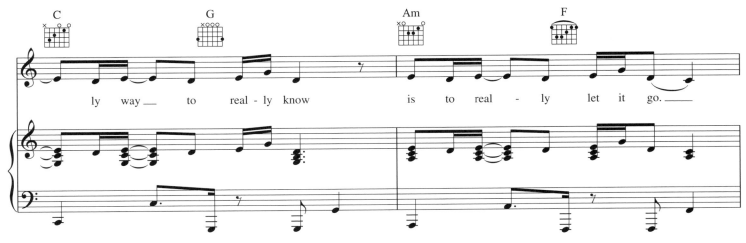

ly way ___ to real - ly know is to real - ly let it go. ___

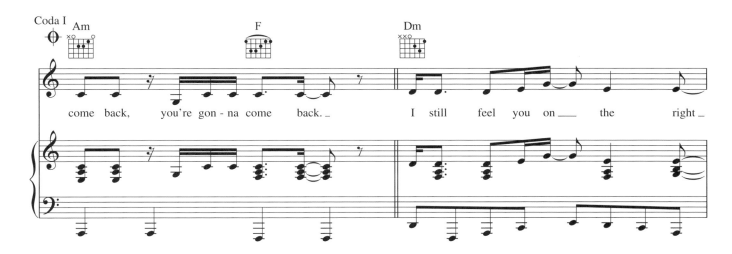

Coda I

come back, you're gon-na come back. __ I still feel you on __ the right __

__ side __ of the bed. __ And I still feel you in __ the blan -

kets pulled o - ver my head. But I'm gon-na wash a - way, __ oh,

I'm gon-na wash a - way __ ev-'ry-thing __ till you __ come home __ to me.

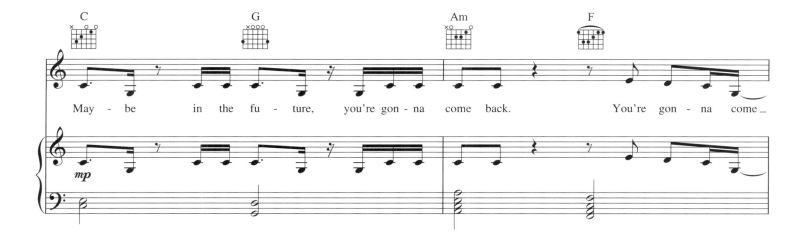

Maybe in the fu - ture, you're gon - na come back. You're gon - na come _

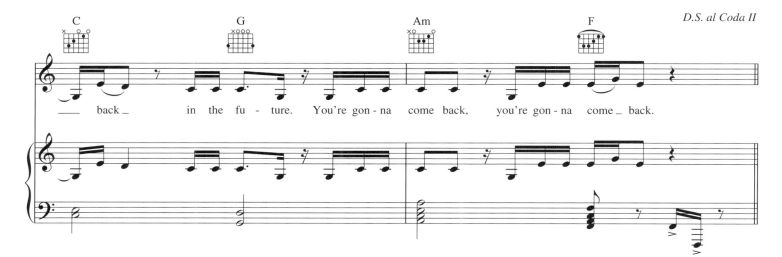

*D.S. al Coda II*

_ back _ in the fu - ture. You're gon - na come back, you're gon - na come _ back.

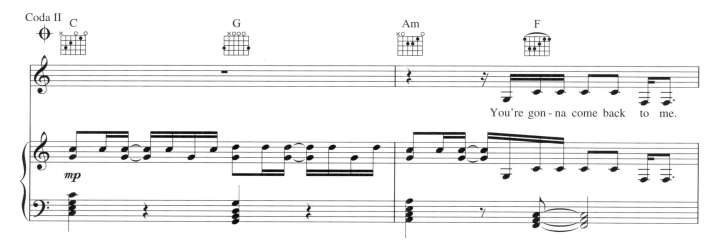

Coda II

You're gon - na come back to me.

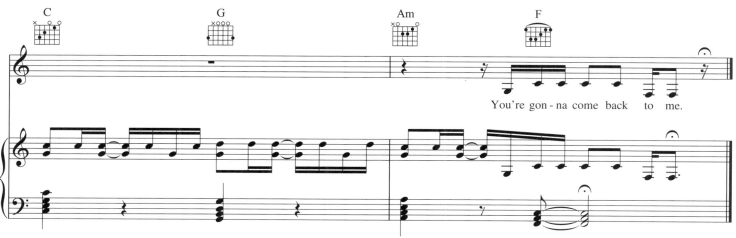

You're gon - na come back to me.